Congratulations on your graduation!

For the graduate I once was,
and for you, dear little graduate, let's celebrate YOU!
Junia Wonders

To my mother and father, who always pushed me to reach for the stars!
Clarissa Corradin

Stars are scattered
throughout this book.
Can you find all of them?

Published by Gmür Verlag
Let's Celebrate You! A Graduation Keepsake for Little Graduates copyright © Gmür Verlag 2024
Text copyright © Junia Wonders 2024
Cover, internal design, and illustrations copyright © Gmür Verlag 2024
All rights reserved.

ISBN 978-3-907130-33-9

www.juniawonders.com

Let's Celebrate YOU!

A Graduation Keepsake
for Little Graduates

Junia Wonders

Illustrated by
Clarissa Corradin

Today is a day worth celebrating.
Look how far you've come—
from the very first steps you took
to the graduate you've become!

You came to class each day
and did your **homework**, too.
You took the tests and passed,
and oh, how *time just flew!*

Your **teachers** taught you lessons
and showed you what to do.
It gave them **joy** to bring out
the very **best** in you.

You listened to your teachers
and learned the Golden Rule.
You followed the routine
they set for **you** at school.

You learned how to make **friends**
by being nice and kind.
Saying **"please"** and **"thank you"**
is always in your mind.

At playtime, you played **fair**,
and let others have a go.
You learned that **taking turns**
and **teamwork** help you grow.

Perhaps you played some sport
and practiced with your team.
With every step you took,
you marched toward your dream.

Win or lose, you **carried on**
with a gracious attitude.
You learned from your mistakes
with a heart of gratitude.

When things got hard at school,
you didn't just give up.
You simply **kept on going**
until you reached the top.

And the top you have reached, **dear graduate!**
That's where you are now.
Let's celebrate your achievement—
go on and take a bow.

There'll be another **mountain**,
another **hill** to climb,
but that's not for today.
That's for another time.

Today is **your day**,
and this much is true:
You've done all the work.
Now, let's celebrate YOU!

Congratulations!
Happy Graduation!

My Graduation Day Memories

My name is _____.

I am _____ years old.

Your graduation photo here!

Your graduation photo here!

On this day, _____,

I graduated from _____.

Today I feel _____.

What I want to remember about today: _____.

Congratulations to the Class of _____!

Your class photo here!

If you are ready,
  as ready as can be,
    you will smile at the future
    and meet it with glee.

—Have You Ever Wondered What You Will Be?
Special Graduation Edition
by Junia Wonders

Let's Celebrate You!

When I grow up, I want...

to be a/an _____

to work _____

to learn _____

to see _____

to play _____

to visit _____

to discover _____

to help _____

to be good at _____

to stay curious about _____

to explore _____

to be successful at _____

It's never too early,
it's never too soon
to wonder what you will be
and aim for the moon.

—*Have You Ever Wondered What You Will Be?*
Special Graduation Edition
by Junia Wonders

Graduation Wishes From Classmates, Teachers, Friends, and Family

Whatever path you take,
   whichever road you choose,
      you will give it your best shot,
   you've got nothing to lose.

—*Have You Ever Wondered What You Will Be?*
Special Graduation Edition
by Junia Wonders

Have You Ever Wondered What You Will Be?

Have you ever **wondered**
what you will be?
When you look in the mirror,
what do you see?

Do you **dream** of things
that seem out of reach?
Do you **daydream** a lot
when you're out on the beach?

Have you ever wondered
what you will be?
When you look at the night sky,
what do you see?

Do you gaze at the stars
and wonder out loud
how to be **special,**
to stand out in a crowd?

For you may be little,
as little as can be,
but someday you will **grow**
like a seedling into a tree.

And you may be small,
as small as you are,
but someday you will **shine**
as bright as a **star.**

Have you ever wondered
what you will be?
When you look **deep inside**,
what do you see?

Do you see your **potential**,
how special you are?
Do you know there's **no doubt**
that you will go far?

—An excerpt from
Have You Ever Wondered What You Will Be?
Special Graduation Edition
by Junia Wonders

Books by Junia Wonders

A timeless and inspiring gift for
any hopeful youngster!

Special Graduation Edition
(includes extra pages for graduates)

A wonderful and
whimsical autumn tale!

A sweet tale about unconditional love!

An adorable rhyming tale of bravery and
hygiene—with a little sprinkle of magic!

A charming rhyming tale of
friendship and sharing!

The **paperback** and **hardcover** editions are available
on Amazon and Barnes&Noble.

Join *Junia's* VIP list at **www.juniawonders.com** for exclusive giveaways.

Made in the USA
Coppell, TX
10 April 2024

31105295R00021